First Printing, 2020
Published in Canada by Lithos Kids Press
Printed in China

ISBN 978-1-989975-04-6

For more books, resources, and a study guide, visit our website:
www.LithosKids.com

We love seeing pictures and artwork from kids! If you have an 'Little Pilgrim' drawings you'd like to share, send them to info@lithoskids.com

You can also purchase more copies of Little Pilgrim's Big Journey and this coloring book at:

www.lithoskids.com